PACKWOOD HOUSE

Warwickshire

THE NATIONAL TRUST

Acknowledgements

This new guidebook by Jeffrey Haworth is heavily indebted to those written jointly by the late Sir Joshua Rowley and James Lees-Milne in 1947, and rewritten by Carew Wallace in 1966 and Major Grundy in 1980. Mr Wallace acknowledged help from the late R. F. Gibling's notes and from the Warwickshire County Record Office. The National Trust would like to thank Charles Nugent for his helpful advice.

Bibliography

Anon., 'Packwood House, Birmingham', *Country Life*, 4 January 1902, pp. 16–24; J. J. Belton, *The Story of Packwood*, 1951; John Cornforth, *The Inspiration of the Past: Country House Taste in the Twentieth Century*, 1985; M. W. Farr, 'The Fetherstons at Packwood in the Seventeenth Century', *Dugdale Society*, occasional paper no. 18, 1968; Michael Hall, 'Packwood House, Warwickshire', *Country Life*, 19 October 1989, pp. 108–13; Christopher Hussey, 'Packwood House, Warwickshire', *Country Life*, 9 and 16 August 1924, pp. 218–24 and 250–7; Margaret Jourdain, 'Packwood House and its Collection', *Apollo*, January and February 1946; C. Lines, 'Who was Baron Ash?', *Warwickshire and Worcestershire Life*, September 1984; H. C. Marillier, *English Tapestries of the 18th Century*, 1930; Jeremy Musson, *The English Manor House*, 1999; J. C. Shepherd and G. A. Jellicoe, *Gardens and Design*, 1927; Roy Strong, *The Renaissance Garden in England*, 1979, pp. 211–14; C. E. C. Tattershall, *A History of British Carpets*, 1934; Geoffrey Tyack, *Warwickshire Country Houses*, 1994, pp. 158–61.

Photographs: courtesy of Colonel Richard Arden Close p. 27; Country Life Picture Library p. 29; courtesy of Captain and Mrs Fetherston-Dilke p. 26; National Trust pp. 8, 32; National Trust Photographic Library p. 22; NTPL/Andreas von Einsiedel pp. 1, 5 (bottom), 9, 10, 11 (bottom left), 12, 13, 14, 17, 18, 19, 21, 31, back cover; NTPL/John Hammond pp. 7, 11 (top right), 15, 16, 20, 28, 30; NTPL/Derek Harris pp. 24–5; NTPL/Keith Hewitt p. 5 (top); NTPL/Roger Hickman front cover, p. 24 (bottom left); NTPL/Stephen Robson p. 4.

Registered charity no. 205846
Revised 2002, 2006; reprinted 2003, 2008
ISBN 978-1-84359-037-8

Typeset from disc and designed by James Shurmer (04 08)

Printed by BAS for National Trust (Enterprises) Ltd, Heelis, Kemble Drive, Swindon, Wiltshire SN2 2NA on stock made from 75% recycled fibre

(*Front cover*) The Yew Garden

(*Title-page*) An early 18th-century embroidered chair in the Great Hall

(*Back cover*) The Ireton Bathroom

CONTENTS

PACKWOOD HOUSE

The neighbouring manor houses of Baddesley Clinton and Packwood could hardly be more sharply contrasting. At Baddesley, the stone house arranged round a courtyard has been unchanged for centuries, moated and hidden away: at Packwood the compact house, relatively undistinguished externally, is a 1920s and '30s recasting of a much altered late 16th-century timber-framed building. It is set off by subsidiary buildings and garden walls in richly coloured brickwork of the 17th century, some of it moulded and architecturally enriched. Furthermore, its setting is public and accessible, the handsome outbuildings putting on a smart face either side of the road, in the way fashionable until the early 18th century. Discovering it suddenly, after a bend in one of the many narrow, erratic lanes characteristic of this unspoilt part of Warwickshire, is an experience never forgotten: one is intrigued and impressed as a traveller three centuries ago would have been. Most fascinating of all are the tantalising glimpses of the yew garden which presents its flank to the public road.

This garden is Packwood's rarest and most famous feature – a representation of the Sermon on the Mount. Its focus is that scarce survival of a pre-1700 garden, a spiral mount, here planted with a magnificent yew known as the Master. Flanking it are a dozen yews said to represent the disciples. Beneath them is the multitude, yews replacing an orchard in the 19th century.

The Sermon is believed to have been planted by John Fetherston, a lawyer, who also built the brick service wing about 1660, a notable example of 'artisan mannerist' work, a style usually associated with Dutch gables. The moulded brick makes use of pilasters, cornices, ovals and roundels, supplemented by sundials.

Packwood is less well known for the immense

The Yew Garden

Packwood from the east – the view from the road

care lavished in repairing, restoring and adding to the buildings and garden by Mr Graham Baron Ash ('Baron' was a Christian name, not a title). For a man fascinated by all things Shakespearean, Packwood was perfect. It stands deep in Shakespeare's Forest of Arden and dates from that era. Baron Ash chose as his architect a man who had restored Shakespeare's birthplace in Stratford, and he filled the house with 17th-century furniture and fittings, some of which have a Shakespearean connection. And every summer he put on performances of Shakespeare's plays in the garden.

Baron Ash gave Packwood House, together with some 45.7 hectares (113 acres), to the National Trust in 1941 in memory of his parents. In addition, he gave his collection of furniture, tapestries and works of art, much of it rescued from Baddesley Clinton. In making this generous gift, Baron Ash was fulfilling his family motto, *Non nobis sed omnibus* – 'not for us but for everyone'.

Baron Ash built the Long Gallery and filled it with old furniture and tapestries

GRAHAM BARON ASH

by James Lees-Milne

I first met Baron Ash in 1931. A pianist friend of mine, a White Russian, George Chavchavadze, gave a concert in the newly erected Great Hall at Packwood. I persuaded my parents to get tickets for the three of us. After the concert and the departure of the audience we stayed behind, were given supper, and made friends. George signed his name on the spinet now in the Drawing Room.

From that day until his death Baron seemed never to change. He was invariably spruce, dressed in well-ironed lounge suits which betrayed that he was not really a countryman. He was infinitely correct, yet not stiff or stuffy. Anxious yet welcoming. A trifle over-sensitive, yet infinitely kind. A very good host, he loved entertaining (his food was always delicious) so long as his guests did not stay too long and were at least half as tidy as himself. For he hated disorder. If one stayed a night at Packwood and left a book lying on a downstairs table it would be removed a minute after one quitted the room. One's unsightly hairbrushes would even be hidden in the drawer of one's dressing-table the moment one descended to breakfast. Yet his manners were impeccable. He was a good companion, liked gossip, so long as it was not scandalous, and laughter. I would say his humour was rudimentary.

Above all he loved old houses and furniture, for which he cultivated a keen and discerning eye. He knew what was genuine and would intuitively detect other people's fakes. Like so many connoisseurs of his generation he was unmoved by Georgian buildings and artefacts; and of course abominated anything Victorian. Yet he knew every pre-classical house within a range of a hundred miles. I do not think paintings, music or works of art generally meant much to him in their own right. He appreciated them as adjuncts to his rooms and life-style.

Packwood was for years the apple of his eye. He made its 'restoration' to what he believed it had originally been his life's task, and filled it with appropriate furniture, tapestries, stained glass and ornaments of great beauty. His romantic side led him to add what had not previously existed, namely the Great Hall and the Long Gallery. And because these annexes were largely contrived from the floors and beams of demolished old houses they became in his eyes genuine apartments. The gardens, too, he resurrected and kept in apple-pie order.

Then came the war of 1939. He was, like every country house owner, obliged to cut staff and entertainment to the bare bone. The long lean years of austerity lessened his interest in the place which he had perfected. When peace returned there was no further room for improvement of his great creation. Besides, he fell in love with a moated castle in Suffolk. Nevertheless the memory of Packwood remained his pride and joy. In presenting it to the National Trust he confidently believed it would be preserved for all time exactly as he left it, that is to say, every stick of furniture and every object would remain in the position in the room in which he had arranged it. If Packwood House looks an immaculate museum today, it was an immaculate museum when Baron lived in it. It never was a proper country house, with worn hats and tobacco pouches in the hall, dogs' baskets and children's toys in the living rooms. Heaven forbid! Baron would have died of horror at the very idea.

(Right) Graham Baron Ash as High Sheriff of Warwickshire; pastel by William Dring, 1943 (Landing)

TOUR OF THE HOUSE

THE HALL

Before being substantially altered by Baron Ash in 1931, the Hall had a light oak balustraded gallery on three sides with a wrought-iron chandelier, both characteristic of the Edwardian era. The wall to the right of the fireplace was still pierced with mullioned windows, and there was frieze-high panelling. This was all swept away, and a new floor of oak from Lymore Park in Montgomeryshire was laid down, with the boards in the long central compartment set in chevron pattern. The timbered ceiling was inserted, and a single gallery of linenfold panelling was built, giving access to the bedrooms on the left from the staircase.

FURNITURE

Oak chest. French, early 16th-century.

Walnut chest, with prominent dovetailing and carrying handles. Italian, 17th-century.

Small oak chest, with sloping top. English, 17th-century.

Painted wrought-iron strong chest. German, 17th-century.

Two Jacobean oak stools, covered in flame-stitch needlework.

Two oak armchairs, the wider one a Yorkshire pattern. English, mid-17th-century.

Walnut tall-back chair, covered in *gros-point* (cross-stitch) needlework, bought in Tours. Late 17th-century.

Oak bookrest incorporating early 16th-century bench-ends (it supports an illustrated commentary on the Bible, Amsterdam, 1721).

Turret clock mechanism, about 300 years old, rescued from the stable loft in the 1980s.

(Opposite page)
The Hall today

(Left)
The Hall in the 1920s, before Baron Ash removed part of the gallery

METALWORK

A variety of bronze mortars, one marked 'ION FRY. ANNO DOMINI: 1684'.

Pair of brass candlesticks. Italian, 17th-century.

Cast-iron 'Armada' fireback, dated 1588.

GLASS

Arms of Queen Elizabeth I and two of her Garter Knights, Thomas Radcliffe, 3rd Earl of Sussex and Thomas Howard, 1st Earl of Suffolk.

PICTURE

After HANS HOLBEIN (*c.*1497–1543)
Henry VIII (1491–1547)
Baron Ash bought this 18th-century copy of the Corsini portrait at Lord Howard of Effingham's sale at Tusmore, Banbury.

TEXTILES

Tapestry, woven with 'Leda and the Swan' and aquatic birds in the background. Brussels, 17th-century. Inscribed 'Jupiter Transformatus' on a cartouche in the border above, as the Roman god Jupiter transformed himself into a swan to rape Leda.

Tapestry, woven with David receiving the sword of Goliath. Flemish, 17th-century.

Tapestry border panel depicting seated female figures, each holding a cross and a book on either side of a landscape with figures. Brussels, early 17th-century.

Sheldon tapestry panel woven with Judith with the head of Holofernes. In a black and gold frame, this rarity was intended either as a picture or for a cushion. Made at Barcheston, Warwickshire, 1610.

Enter the Long Gallery and turn right into the Parlour.

The Parlour

THE PARLOUR

Character is given to the room by the full-height Jacobean panelling and the mullioned-and-transomed window introduced by Baron Ash. It affords the best view of the 17th-century inner forecourt.

FURNITURE

Walnut chair with spoon-back and cabriole legs (copy of a Queen Anne chair).

Oak gate-leg table. English, 17th-century.

Oak side-table with carved frieze (some adaptation). English, 17th-century.

Oak chest-of-drawers. English, late 17th-century.

Walnut armchair, woven in floral needlework, bought in France. French, late 17th-century.

Walnut chair on cabriole legs, the seat and back covered in needlework. English, early 18th-century.

Oak chair, seat and back covered in needlework dated 1933.

Miniature chair in fruitwood, bamboo pattern. English, 1820s.

Carved figure of Mars, brought from Baddesley Clinton nearby, like much of the contents of Packwood (see p. 30). Early 18th-century.

CLOCK

Red lacquer longcase clock, by Henry Harrison of London. Late 17th-century.

METALWORK

Bronze 'arrow' vase, Chinese.

Cast-iron fireback with arms of Philip II of Spain, husband of Queen Mary Tudor.

PICTURES

JAN VAN KESSEL (1626–79)
Peasants carousing outside an Inn
Formerly belonged to Lady Manton, of Offchurch Bury, Warwickshire.

Formerly attributed to PHILIPS WOUWERMANS (1619–68)
Landscape with Figures
Probably bought at Lord Howard of Effingham's sale at Tusmore, Banbury.

18th-century Neapolitan crib figures in the Parlour

Baron Ash commissioned new needlework to match his older furnishings

TEXTILES

A verdure (foliage) tapestry woven with a lion and a griffin fighting. Brussels, late 17th-century.

DOLLS

Doll group: A woman with a black pageboy, from a religious display. Italian, 18th-century.

STAINED GLASS

The painted roundels in the window are all 17th-century. The circular panel of Adam and Eve, dated 1682, came from Combe Abbey in Warwickshire, which lost much of its artistic and decorative interest in the 1920s.

THE LONG GALLERY

It was a stroke of genius on Baron Ash's part to join the two great halls together by that most Elizabethan of features, a long gallery. Visually, it is a triumph, with the light – from one side of the room only – striking highly polished old oak and the rich patterning of old tapestry. As a result, perhaps it does not matter that the architecture is pedestrian and stolid. Sir Nikolaus Pevsner thought the outside resembled a grammar school. What Baron Ash was doing was original and innovative, and his architect, Edwin Reynolds, of the local firm, Wood, Kendrick & Reynolds, had considerable experience remodelling historic buildings such as Aston Hall and Blakesley Hall. But Reynolds may have found it difficult to assert himself with such a demanding client who acted as his own clerk-of-works.

The walnut chairs, c.1700, are covered with English flame-stitch needlework

DECORATION

The wide, long oak floorboards are from Lymore Park and the panelling from Shaftsmoor, Hall Green, Birmingham. In both cases, the fittings were rescued from buildings being pulled down. The fireplace is from Chipping Norton in Oxfordshire, but the overmantel came from Shaftsmoor.

FURNITURE

'Nonsuch' chest inlaid with holly and bog oak. The marquetry shows eccentric turrets which resemble those of Henry VIII's Nonsuch Palace in Surrey, demolished in the late 17th century. English, 16th-century.

East Indian chest on stand, lacquered in black and gold. Early 19th-century. Such chests are usually much plainer, like the pair flanking the hall fireplace at Hanbury Hall in Worcestershire.

Oak chest with moulded and panelled front, inlaid with bone and mother-of-pearl. English, *c.*1650–75.

Walnut chairs, *c.*1700, covered with English flame-stitch needlework.

Longcase clock in tortoiseshell lacquered case with chinoiserie designs. The movement is by John Wood, Grantham. English, 18th-century.

METALWORK

Chinese bronze silk iron, *bronze bell*, with banded decoration, *English bell-metal cauldron*, and *cast-iron fireback with figure of Neptune.*

CERAMICS

Chinese porcelain wine pot in the form of a duck, *continental peasant dish with splashed coloured glazes*, and *Swiss green-glazed jar and cover.*

STAINED GLASS

The roundel of a pilgrim is 16th-century, the remainder 17th-century.

TAPESTRIES

WINDOW WALL, OPPOSITE DOOR TO PARLOUR:

The Coronation of Marcus Aurelius. Woven in the Antwerp workshop of Michel Wauters *c.*1655–70. Bought from the Baddesley Clinton sales in the 1930s. Next to it is another, possibly from the same set.

The Long Gallery was built in 1931–2 to connect two existing halls

FLANKING GARDEN DOOR:

Fragments showing a shepherd and a shepherdess. Mortlake, English, early 18th-century.

END WALL NEXT TO DOOR TO GREAT HALL:

Fragment showing figures of a man wearing a helmet and a woman. Flemish, early 16th-century.

ALONG LONG WALL:

Verdure tapestry woven with a bird and a house, Brussels.

St Remy crowning Charles VII before Joan of Arc. To bolster French resistance to the English, Joan persuaded Charles to be crowned king in Rheims in 1429. The fellow panel to this is in the Treasury at Rouen Cathedral. Aubusson, French, early 17th-century.

FLANKING FIREPLACE:

Fragment woven with a figure of Rachel, Jacob's wife, surrounded by children. There is a complete version of this tapestry depicting the *Reconciliation of Jacob and Esau* in the Museum of Applied Arts at Budapest. Brussels, late 16th-century.

Copernicus and the Elements. Brussels, 17th-century. Copernicus was the founder of modern astronomy.

TO RIGHT OF PARLOUR DOORWAY:

Verdure tapestry, woven with birds in a landscape. Bought by Ash in Tournai. Flemish, 16th-century.

END WALL, NEXT TO DOOR TO ENTRANCE HALL:

Fragment showing a woman offering a drink to a man (Rebecca and Eliezer). Brussels, 17th-century.

THE GREAT HALL

Formerly detached from the house and used as a cow-byre and barn, the Great Hall was fashioned in its present shape in 1924–7. A sprung floor for dancing was installed, and the hayrack adapted into a balustrade for the gallery.

FIREPLACE

The stone fireplace and plaster overmantel came out of an old wine shop in the High Street, Stratford-upon-Avon, belonging to John Smith and his wife Margaret. Both date from Shakespeare's day, and indeed the playwright may well have sat in front of them. The overmantel bears the initials of the Smith family, and the stone lintel of the fireplace two small barrels to indicate their trade. The fireback is of the pattern known as 'Royal Oak', commemorating the oak tree at Boscobel in which Charles II hid during his escape from England in 1651.

DECORATION

The upper crucks supporting the roof spring from corbels modelled on originals at Carcasonne in south-west France.

Baron Ash's devotion to the Royal Family may have prompted him to base the design of his new semicircular oriel window on that in the royal palace of Hampton Court. In front of it, tea was laid for Queen Mary on her visit on 23 August 1927, accompanied by her lady-in-waiting, Lady Bradford of Castle Bromwich Hall. Queen Mary's coat of arms was installed in the window, with her permission, to commemorate the occasion.

Pre-war photographs show the great table placed against the tapestries in the Long Gallery, while sofas flanked the Great Hall fireplace to make a comfortable sitting-room. It was kept warm by the efficient new central-heating system, which is still in use, run from a stylish boiler room reminiscent of the engine room of a liner.

FURNITURE

Oak refectory table, 6.4 metres long. The distinctive Jacobean-pattern supports are early 17th-century, though the plank top is believed to be earlier. It is the principal treasure Baron Ash was able to buy from Cecil Ferrers at Baddesley Clinton in the 1930s. It is recorded that two related benches were thrown out and burnt at Baddesley in 1870.

The Great Hall

Set of six early 18th-century English walnut chairs, the knees of the cabriole legs carved with acanthus leaves. The floral *gros-point* needlework to the backs and seats belonged to Lady Penelope Street, daughter of Sir Roland Berkeley, and is mentioned in her will in 1709. Baron Ash bought the chairs from a Mr Robinson in Warwick, who got them at Christie's in November 1928.

Set of four walnut chairs, the back and seats covered in Utrecht velvet (a woollen velvet), the survival of which is a great rarity. Italian, late 17th-century.

Oak bench, elaborately carved. In the style of the late 17th-century designer Daniel Marot. Flemish, late 17th-century.

Sedan chair, covered in leather. Inside is an 18th-century dressed dummy figure of a lady holding a fan. French. From Baddesley Clinton.

So-called 'Act of Parliament' clock by Robert Haines,

Oxford. He is recorded as working *c.*1775. Such clocks were hung in inns, and were once thought to have been inspired by the 1797 Act which taxed private watches and clocks.

METALWORK

Bronze imperial bushel measure dated 1826. Inscribed 'Mrs Jane Lewin, Halesworth Manor'.

PICTURES

ENGLISH, early 18th-century
Wilson Aylesbury Roberts as a Boy
From Aylesbury House, Hockley Heath. The background was repainted later.

ENGLISH, mid-17th-century
An Unknown Girl with an Ostrich Feather Hat
From Baddesley Clinton.

The figures in the foreground of this c.1733 Soho tapestry symbolise Africa. Baron Ash bought it from nearby Baddesley Clinton in the 1930s

The framed coats of arms above the tapestries are known as hatchments, which were traditionally displayed outside a house on the death of its owner. They include, over the fireplace, that of Baron Ash, who died on 20 February 1980.

ARMORIAL GLASS

By Messrs Pearce & Cutler, Bridge Street, Broad Street, Birmingham. Mostly 1921.

Far gable window: Henry VIII

Gallery gable window: Catherine of Aragon

OPPOSITE FIREPLACE, LEFT TO RIGHT:

The Warwickshire families of Bolding, Wade, Ash, Holroyd, Ludlow and Ferrers.

Oriel window: Ireton, Charles II, Elizabeth I and Fetherston. The lower arms are Queen Mary's.

TEXTILES

BY ENTRANCE DOOR:

Portière (door curtain) of coloured appliqué work. Portuguese.

OPPOSITE FIREPLACE:

Tapestry depicting two scenes from the story of Saul. Brussels, 16th-century.

END WALL:

Tapestry showing a sacrificial lamb from the same series as the previous tapestry. Brussels, 16th-century. Both tapestries were bought recently from Aske Hall, Richmond, Yorkshire.

FLANKING FIREPLACE:

The Continent of Africa, originally part of a double panel. Africa is represented by a white princess wearing a feathered headdress, while an attendant black woman holds out an armadillo. Soho, England, *c.*1733. Bought from Baddesley Clinton. Based on a design by L. van Schoor.

Terraced water garden tapestry with muses in the foreground. Brussels, late 17th-century. This tapestry was formerly in the Great Parlour at Baddesley Clinton.

Silk damask banners. Used by Baron Ash when he was High Sheriff of Warwickshire in 1938–9.

THE STAIRCASE AND LANDINGS

This rather harsh form of staircase, made in 1931–2, may be a product of the very limited space available, but it is still surprising that Baron Ash resisted importing an antique example salvaged from a demolished building – a wide selection must have been available to him.

PICTURES

ANTONIO VERRIO (1639–1707)
Charles II (1630–85)
On plaster
This is a rare fragment from the ceiling of the King's Drawing Room at Windsor Castle, which was destroyed during Sir Jeffry Wyatville's alterations in the early 19th century. Verrio was the leading mural painter of the late 17th century.

Mary, Queen of Scots (1542–87)
A near copy, probably 19th-century, of a portrait at Hardwick Hall in Derbyshire.

TAPESTRIES

Men and women conversing. Found stored in a box at Baddesley Clinton. Brussels, 17th-century.

Animals disporting among trees. Flemish, late 16th-century.

Part panel woven with figures embarking in boats. Brussels, late 17th-century.

THE FETHERSTON BEDROOM

This room used to be Baron Ash's bedroom, though no furniture exists to furnish it, as he took this with him when he moved to Wingfield Castle.

THE IRETON BATHROOM

This combines the up-to-date luxury of bath and basin and chromium-plated fittings with the pre-war passion for Delft tiles. Besides Holland, Bristol and Liverpool were major 18th-century producers of such tiles. The bath and surround has 407 whole tiles and 63 part tiles.

The linoleum floor was badly pockmarked by visitors' shoes during the craze for stiletto heels, before the National Trust took steps to protect its houses from such forms of damage.

THE IRETON ROOM

By repute, the Parliamentary general Henry Ireton slept here before the Battle of Edgehill in 1642, the opening engagement of the English Civil War. (Packwood is as inconveniently placed for Edgehill as Owlpen is for Tewkesbury.)

FURNITURE

Tester bed with massive turned pillars. English, early 17th-century. The curtains and bedspread are early 18th-century English crewelwork.

Two single chairs, one with back and seat in 'Turkey-work' (English knotted needlework pile), the other with unusual fan-shaped crest rail. English, mid-17th-century.

The Ireton Bedroom. The Parliamentary general Henry Ireton is supposed to have slept here

THE CENTRAL LANDING

PICTURES

CHARLES-FRANÇOIS LACROIX DE MARSEILLE (*c.*1700–82)
Coastal Scene
Lacroix was a studio assistant of Claude-Joseph Vernet and produced views of this kind in his style.

WILLIAM DRING, RA (1904–90)
Graham Baron Ash (1889–1980), 1943
Wearing court dress as High Sheriff of Warwickshire (1938–9).

CHINESE, 18th-century
Courtyard Scene, ?Imperial Palace, Peking
Survey of the 'Manours of Packwood and Knowle', 1723.

At the far end of the Inner Landing is Queen Mary's Room.

QUEEN MARY'S ROOM

The bathroom opening out of this bedroom was put at Queen Mary's disposal on her visit in 1927.

The distinctive feature of the bedroom is the late 17th-century panelling, believed to be original to the room. The type, with large flat panels bounded by a simple moulding, is less flamboyant than the bolder style which succeeded it at the end of the century.

Queen Mary's Room commemorates the Queen's visit in 1927

September: one of the 16th-century Flemish stained-glass roundels in Queen Mary's Room

FURNITURE

Chest-of-drawers, walnut-veneered, the top and front inlaid with seaweed marquetry. English, early 18th-century.

Bedstead hung with old Italian green watered silk, much faded.

Two walnut-veneered chairs, one with shells carved on the knees of the cabriole legs, the other with acanthus carving. English, early 18th-century.

Miniature furniture: oak table and pair of Louis XV miniature *bergère* armchairs.

Gilt-framed wall mirror. English, early 18th-century.

Longcase clock. Italian, early 18th-century.

CERAMICS

Pair of Capo di Monte groups, representing Africa and America. Baron Ash bought them because of their connection with the emblems in the Soho tapestry of Africa in the Great Hall (and the companion tapestry of America, since stolen).

PICTURES

Formerly attributed to Sir PETER LELY (1618–80)
Lord Rochester (1647–80)
Wild liver, and author of biting satires and frank lyric poetry.

ENGLISH, early 18th-century
Rustic Scene outside an Inn

Queen Mary (1867–1953)
Photograph taken by Baron Ash during the Queen's visit in 1927.

STAINED GLASS

The roundels are mostly religious subjects. Flemish, 16th-century.

THE LOOKOUT ROOM

From here you get the best panoramic view over the garden. Framed views relating to Packwood include an 1868 tinted lithograph (when the house belonged to John Fetherston, FSA) and two designs made in the 1920s for reinstating the missing half-timbering, which strike a bogus note: they were never carried out. On the walls are a series of archival photographs showing the development of the garden from 1868 to the first quarter of the 20th century.

QUEEN MARGARET'S ROOM

The room is named after the bed, the oak bedstock of which is said to have been slept in by Margaret of Anjou (wife of Henry VI) before the Battle of Tewkesbury (4 May 1471), where she led the Lancastrian army. The pillars and canopy are much later and upholstered in a light woollen material with red braiding. Bought by Baron Ash at the sale of the contents of Owlpen Manor, Gloucestershire, in 1927.

FURNITURE

Two William-and-Mary chests-of-drawers. The tall one has three secret drawers. The drawers of the lower chest are lined with a very rare contemporary block-printed paper featuring royal crowns and symbols of the four seasons.

Longcase clock by John Verow, Hinckley. English, mid-18th-century.

TEXTILES

The canvas wall-hangings, a very rare survival of what is known as 'poor man's tapestry', illustrate the

Queen Margaret's Room is named after Henry VI's Queen, who is said to have slept in this bed in 1471

fables of La Fontaine. It is unclear whether they also came from Owlpen, which was once rich in such textiles. English, ?early 18th-century.

Walk back down the stairs to the ground floor, cross the Hall, and turn right in the Screens Passage.

THE INNER HALL

This was the entrance hall until the drive across the causeway in the park was given up in the 19th century. The original timber framing was revealed when the Edwardian panelling was removed.

TEXTILES

Woven panel depicting Rachel and Leah. Probably a table carpet, it was bought from Baddesley Clinton where it was found in a box. Dutch, early 17th-century.

FURNITURE

Apart from the two plain chests, the furniture is all English, mid-17th-century.

METALWORK

Cast-metal helmet cresting, possibly from over a tomb. 16th-century.

Fireback showing Christ and the woman of Samaria.

PICTURES

Madonna and Child
Labelled 'French, early 17th century', but appears to be a copy of a 16th-century Flemish mannerist painting.

ENGLISH, early 17th-century
Woman with a Carnation

THE DRAWING ROOM

The fireplace, panelling and ceiling beams appear to be features original to the house, implying a Jacobean date for its origin.

FURNITURE

Walnut day-bed. English, *c.*1650–75.

Chest on stand, veneered with walnut and ebony, inlaid with seaweed marquetry. English, early 18th-century.

Spinet by Thomas Hitchcock the Younger. English, *c.*1690.

Walnut wing armchair, covered in yellow brocatelle, used by Queen Mary on her visit in 1927. English, early 18th-century.

Pole-screen with gros-point and petit-point needlework panel representing a house in a formal garden. English, mid-18th-century.

Longcase clock by Edward Eyston, late 17th-century.

CERAMICS

Green glazed group of a Sage with attendants. Chinese, Ming dynasty (1368–1644).

Rockingham cup and saucer, used by Queen Mary.

A mid-18th-century firescreen in the Drawing Room

PICTURES

After PETER PAUL RUBENS (1577–1640)
Philip IV of Spain on horseback
A free copy of a lost original.

ANON, 17th-century
Portraits of an Unknown Man and Woman

STAINED GLASS

Figures of saints within floral borders. Brought from Culham House, Oxfordshire, in 1935. Possibly previously at Christ Church Cathedral, Oxford. Flemish, early 17th-century.

THE STUDY

The Jacobean panelling appears to be the original.

FURNITURE

The two cane-seated chairs are English, *c.*1650–75.

METALWORK

The fireback is English, dated 1635.

CERAMICS

Worcester tea service with black husk decoration. English, late 18th-century.

PICTURES

The portraits were bought in Birmingham as of Henrietta Maria and 'Minette', the mother and sister of Charles II respectively. Attributed to Theodore Russel (1614–88/9), who painted a series of similar portraits at Warwick Castle.

STAINED GLASS

The roundels are also from Culham House. Flemish, early 17th-century.

Next to the front door is the Dining Room.

The Dining Room

THE DINING ROOM

This room has been much altered: the fireplace has been moved from the corner of the room, but the moulded ceiling beams are original.

FURNITURE

Oak double gate-leg table. English, 17th-century.

Six walnut chairs and a day-bed, all with cane backs and seats. English, *c.*1650–75.

Oak cupboard inlaid with bone and mother-of-pearl and decorated with split balusters. This especially high-quality piece is from Baddesley Clinton. English, late 17th-century.

Two 18th-century armchairs in flame-stitch needlework.

TEXTILES

A large flame-stitch hanging. English, *c.*1700.

SILVER

Tankard with repoussé flowers. London, 1747.

Plate with dragoon edge. Silver gilt, by Wakelin and Parker. London, 1773.

Silver-gilt salver with Ash arms. Birmingham, 1899.

Eighteen-inch salver with Ash armorials. London, 1934.

Half-size copy of the Dolben Cup. London, 1934. The original, made in 1678, is probably the largest and finest porringer (shallow bowl) of its type.

PICTURE

Manner of Sir GODFREY KNELLER (1646/9–1723)
Aylesbury Roberts and Anne Aylesbury
From Aylesbury House nearby.

THE GARDEN

In 1927 the garden designer Geoffrey Jellicoe wrote:

Packwood is essentially English. It has that want of a complete unified plan (for the group of buildings that embrace the road are the result of accident as much as design) that seems to characterise English work; it plays with the most beautiful materials; and, above all, it has a worldliness combined with a curious vague, indefinable mysticism that seems to be somehow inherent in the northern race. The garden mainly lies south-east of the house, and is a direct throw-back to earlier days. It is entered from the house or by a door in the wall from the forecourt and from that moment, owing to the slight stage-like rise in the ground, the whole garden lies outstretched. In the foreground is the rectangular flower garden, its corners once enclosing four little garden houses. The small raised terrace so reminiscent of earlier days separates this from what lies behind: yews and mysticism. It is the story of the Sermon on the Mount. Step into this medley and its idea takes us back to the days when the teaching of the Church held its sway over the human mind.

The 18th-century gates were set up in the Carolean Garden by Baron Ash in 1935

The lawyer who planted these yews must have been a disciple of Milton. When we pass up the central way we are passing through the strange diverse shapes of the multitude; at the top are the twelve apostles with the four evangelists in the centre; and on the Mount is the tree symbolising the Teacher. Reached by a spiral path after such an impressive journey, the arbour in the tree must have been, and remains, a place for deepest meditation. Over the garden there would have been heard the buzzing of the bees whose hives were contained in the holes of the terrace wall; the orchard along the west boundary brings us back to today; and the great elms remind us of the freshness of country that lies beyond.

The elms have gone, but the rest remains.

TOUR OF THE GARDEN

THE SOUTH OR CAROLEAN GARDEN

Through a wrought-iron gate lies the South or Carolean Garden. Of the gazebos at its four corners, that in the north-east dates from the 1660s–70s. It incorporates a fireplace and a horizontal flue used to heat the adjacent south-facing wall on which peaches were grown. That at the west end of the Terrace Walk is probably early 18th-century. The north-west one has been rebuilt exactly in the style shown in a drawing of 1756 at Maxstoke Castle, while that in the south-east corner at the other end of the terrace is modern, though built on the foundations of an earlier one.

THE DOUBLE HERBACEOUS BORDERS

The layout of the Carolean Garden has undergone significant change in recent years, with the re-instatement of the gravel path system, crisscrossing the garden and its accompanying herbaceous borders. This marks a return to the 19th- and early 20th-century arrangement, illustrated in Geoffrey Jellicoe's plan of the garden from 1927, and restores a valuable chapter of the garden's history. The area in front of the house had remained as lawn since the Second World War when labour shortages made the existing parterre scheme impossible to maintain.

The decision to reinstate this scheme was taken in 2004, after lengthy consultation between the gardeners, historic buildings and gardens advisers and the National Trust Gardens Panel. It was decided that the return to this older, Victorian layout, as opposed to Baron Ash's parterre scheme, would offer the most desirable and practical way to bring this area back to life. The scheme finally restored the link between the house and the Yew Garden discernible in all the garden's previous incarnations from the 18th century until the Second World War. It was also the arrangement present for much of the Ashes' time at Packwood and offers a practical solution to the wear and tear caused by Packwood's increasing visitor numbers.

Work was completed over the two winters between 2005 and 2006. The path is constructed of Breedon gravel with custom-made steel edging and a narrow grass to edging strip. As no original plant lists for the borders exist, the planting seeks to follow the feel of surviving photos, whilst building on Packwood's tradition of 'mingled' planting.The spiky silhouettes of *Yucca recurvifolia* provide a year-round structure to the border, as do *Euphorbia characias* and the grass *Stipa gigantea*, while hardy herbaceous plants in a restrained palette of blues, silvers and magenta give a long season of display.

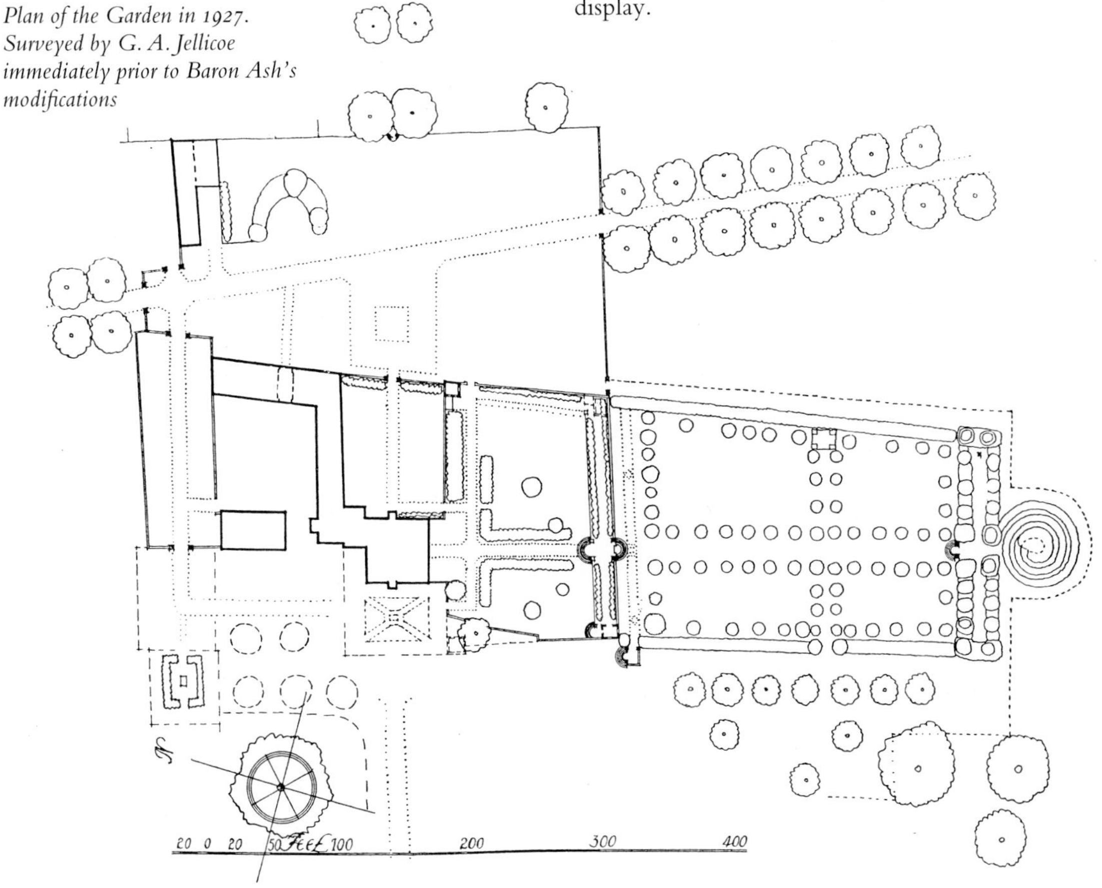

Plan of the Garden in 1927. Surveyed by G. A. Jellicoe immediately prior to Baron Ash's modifications

THE MAIN BORDER

Long known as the Yellow Border, this is crammed full of closely planted herbaceous perennials in riotously mixed colours. It is perhaps the best example of Packwood's use of the mingled style of planting, where small groups or single plants are repeated at intervals along the length of a border with an emphasis on flower over form. This style is described by the eminent 19th-century garden writer J. C. Loudon in his 1822 *Encyclopaedia of Gardening* and has been perpetuated through the years by successive head gardeners at Packwood.

As the border can reach in excess of seven feet in height, staking is an essential task. This is carried out in spring with pea sticks cut from the local woods and inserted in the ground throughout the border.

THE SUNKEN GARDEN

The Sunken Garden was constructed in its present form by Baron Ash, as were the Rose Bays along the roadside wall. Red *Rosa* 'Lilli Marlene' alternates with yellow *R.* 'Bright Smile' in the bays, while on the wall creamy yellow 'Leverkusen' alternates with red *R.* 'Dortmund'.

The Yew Garden

THE TERRACE WALK

An elliptical flight of steps leads from the gravel path between a pair of lower piers with stone vases, on to a narrow, raised walk between billowing planting.

The borders were redeveloped at the beginning of this century and are densely planted with a mixture of richly coloured hardy and frost-tender plants in Packwood's characteristic mingled style. Rich, hot colours provide a dramatic contrast to the sombre silhouette of the Yew Garden beyond. The structural backbone of the border is provided by the repetition of certain striking plants along its length, notably: the Honey Splurge (*Euphorbia mellifera*), New Zealand flax (*Phormium* 'Bronze Baby'), Pheasant's Tail Grass (*Stipa arundinacea*) and Red-hot Pokers (*Kniphofia* 'Royal Standard'), joined in summer by the purple-flowered Kangaroo Apple (*Solanum laciniatum*), the bronze-leaved Castor Oil Plant (*Ricinus communis* 'Impala') and, perhaps most striking of all, the cabbage-like, black-leaved *Aeonium arboretum* 'Zwartkop').

The use of such a large array of tender plants, biennials and annuals gives these borders a long season of interest, from spring, when the deliciously honey-scented *Euphorbia mellifera* is in flower alongside 'Red Shine' tulips, through early summer with its Red-hot Pokers and oriental poppies, until the display reaches its peak in late summer when the tender dahlias, salvias and fuchsias are in full, riotous flower, an effect that continues until the first autumn frosts blacken the foliage.

From this terrace you pass though the splendid early 18th-century wrought-iron gateway, long painted white, into the Yew Garden.

THE YEW GARDEN

On the south face of the terrace wall are 30 round-headed niches in pairs, built to house a colony of bee-skeps. These are known as bee boles and may be clearly seen in the 1756 drawing (illustrated on p. 26).

Part of this ground was originally set out by John Fetherston, probably between 1650 and 1670, though there is no evidence of the 'Sermon on the

The Terrace Walk

Mount' tradition before the last quarter of the 19th century. Although the estate plan of 1723 shows the lower part of this garden, which is said to represent 'The Multitude', as being planted with trees, there is strong evidence suggesting that the present pattern of yew trees replaced an orchard no earlier than the middle of the 19th century. They certainly look young in early photographs. A central path bounded by laurel, present in 1902, had been removed by 1924, when *Country Life* revisited. This time a neat rustic stone path – later removed by Baron Ash – is shown parallel with the raised walk. At the other end of this lower garden is a raised path, reached by a short flight of steps. This transverse walk is flanked by twelve great yews now known as 'The Apostles' with four very big specimens in the middle known as 'The Evangelists'. Crowning 'The Mount', reached by a spiral path hedged with box and on the axis of the garden, is a single yew tree, 'The Master', also sometimes called 'The Pinnacle of the Temple'. This tree and the twelve trees on the raised terrace probably formed part of John Fetherston's original plan. Some of the yews are now over 15 metres high, and require considerable skill and effort to trim. The yew trees and box hedges are cut once a year, beginning in August. It takes four gardeners 2½ months, using a hydraulic hoist. The result is a sharp contrast between the precision of the 'biblical' yews and the outer hedges, which may take their form partly from distortion by snow and neglect long ago.

Returning across the Carolean Garden, you will see the wrought-iron gates, placed in the west wall in 1935 to commemorate the Silver Jubilee of George V. Beyond is the Victory Vase marking the Battle of Britain.

The west side of the house is reached by passing through a gate in the north wall of this garden.

FOUNTAIN COURT

This side of the house was the main entrance in the 18th century, the causeway of the lake forming the carriage drive to the house. The sundial at the centre of the gravelled court surrounded by yew hedges is one of those put up by John Fetherston and is dated 1667. In the north-west corner of this part of the garden, and also surrounded by a yew hedge, is an interesting cold plunge bath originally built in 1680. Both the water faucet of the bath and the pillar sundial bear the arms of the Fetherston family, who built Packwood and lived here for nearly 300 years.

THE NORTH COURT

The formal entrance for cars was made by the Ash family, replacing pigsties. It featured lead urns and small lead figures, long removed for security reasons. The fountain pool is two metres deep.

The trees north of the drive are limes – *Tilia oliveri*, known as the 'Chinaman's Moustache Lime'. The name comes from the semicircular ring which forms just above the junction of the branch with the main stem.

THE HISTORY OF PACKWOOD

The name is thought to have been derived from the Saxon 'Pacca's Wood', but no traces have been found of the original settlement, if there was one. The earliest mention of the name is in 1190, when 'Walter Chaplain of Packwood' witnessed a deed. Much of the land hereabouts, including Packwood, belonged to the Benedictine monks of Coventry, some fourteen miles away. After the Dissolution of the Monasteries in the 1530s the property changed hands repeatedly, passing first to the Sheldon family and to Robert Burdett of Bramcote, who sold it to John Fetherston for £340 in 1598.

THE FETHERSTONS

The Fetherstons had been living nearby at Knowle since at least 1468, and in 1598 they seem to have moved into a building (later known as Fetherston House) which was not far from the present Packwood House. John Fetherston's father, William, described himself as a 'yeoman', but was an important enough local figure to have contributed towards preparations against the Spanish Armada in 1588. John seems to have built the core of the present Packwood, and the tall gables of his new 'great mansion howse' proclaimed the family's ambitions. William came to live with his son at Packwood in 1599, handing over to him all his goods, bedsteads, tables, cupboards and wall-hangings there. The inventory made on John's death in 1634 suggests that it was furnished like a prosperous farmhouse, with large numbers of pewter plates and brass pots and pans, and a dozen silver spoons. John died a yeoman like his father, but had educated his sons as gentlemen. The eldest, also called John, who inherited the estate, trained as a barrister, while the youngest, Thomas, became a physician.

The Civil War seems to have caused little disturbance, but much heart-searching, in the family. About 1642 John Fetherston wrote to a brother:

Good Brother, I am a distraction concerninge my armor (beinge alltogeither unable to satisfy my self in judgment and conscience what to do) by reason of the

The south front about 1756, before the half-timbering had been removed

severall commands of the Kinge and parliament; my protestation putts me in mind that I am bound in conscience to serve both, and yet there seems now a very great difference betweene them; which I humbly desyer allmightly god, if it be his will, may be peaceably & timely composed and settled for the good of this churche and kingdome.

A balance seems to have been maintained, as before the Battle of Edgehill in 1642 Cromwell's General, Henry Ireton, slept at Packwood in the room called after him, and it is a tradition that Charles II was given refreshment at Packwood after his defeat at the Battle of Worcester in 1651.

With the restoration of Charles II in 1660, John Fetherston seems to have felt confident enough to contemplate further building, as he probably commissioned the L-shaped red-brick stable block and outbuildings in the following decade. He may also have planted the first yews in the garden. In addition, John West erected a timber-framed building of three rooms for him in 1670. John Fetherston died that year, having suffered from gout in his old age (in a notebook, he had recorded a remedy to 'take away the payne and greife' of the illness).

John's son Thomas built the plunge bath in Fountain Court in 1680, and lived quietly at Packwood for the next 34 years. By the turn of the century the estate had grown to over 600 acres, but John seems to have shared his father's cautious nature, trying – unsuccessfully – to avoid serving as sheriff of Warwickshire in 1692, which was an unpopular honour because of the expense it entailed. Thomas died in 1714 without leaving any children, and six years later the estate passed to his great-niece Dorothy, who married Thomas Leigh of Aldridge in Staffordshire the same year. (The Leighs later added Fetherston to their name in recognition of this inheritance.) Their daughter Catherine inherited in 1755 and on her death in 1769 Packwood went to a junior branch of the Dilke family of Maxstoke Castle. Thomas Fetherston-Dilke was probably responsible for covering Packwood's half-timbering with render and inserting the sash-windows in the early 19th century. His brother Charles, who inherited in 1815, was said to have lived 'in the true style of an English gentleman, who seems to feel a patriotic pride in being clad in the produce of his own estate. His hat, coat and under apparel, stockings, etc., and even his shoes, are the produce of his own lands, herds, etc. and are manufactured and made within his own walls.' His daughter Frances produced nine children; they and the extravagance of her husband forced the family to rent out the house from 1851 and move to Knowle, where the last Fetherston squire of Packwood died in 1876.

Packwood from the east in the early 19th century

THE ASH FAMILY

In 1869 Packwood was bought by George Oakes Arton, who seems to have neglected it. In 1902 *Country Life* found 'ancient walls, vested with ivy, clinging to them sometimes in too fond embrace. Grown rank and strong, its huge arms are intertwined with the brickwork, which they have loosened and in part overthrown, and its very trunks have crept through the walls.' On Arton's death in 1904 the house was put up for auction and bought in 1905 by Alfred Ash, father of the donor.

Alfred Ash claimed to have bought Packwood because his son Graham wanted it, although he was then only a sixteen-year-old schoolboy at Radley. Ash and his father Joseph had made the family fortune in the galvanised iron and metal perforation industries, based in Staffordshire and Birmingham. His obituary in 1925 in a sporting journal (he was a racehorse owner) described him as 'a big, rather swarthy man – with a mass of curly hair, who produced that geniality in others which was his own great gift. He viewed life from the sunny side – and from the interior of a gorgeous Rolls-Royce.'

THE CULT OF THE MANOR HOUSE

The young Graham Baron Ash may have first been drawn to Packwood by the romantic photographs of it published in *Country Life* in 1902. Jeremy Musson, the present Architectural Editor of that magazine, describes the appeal of such ancient manor houses to Baron Ash's generation:

> As featured in *Country Life*, [they] represented an expression of idealised views of England's past and, indeed, its present. Such houses showed that it was a peaceful nation, for they were not built for defence but rather habitation. To such people as the Souls and Lord Curzon, the houses represented the upholding of social duties and the social fabric, which for them was the rôle of the aristocracy and landed gentry. To Ruskin, Morris and others, they represented the proud traditions of craftsmanship that had been destroyed by industrialisation.

But the most breathtaking and apparently perfect surviving old manor houses featured in the pages of *Country Life* had mostly been through the process Baron Ash was to carry out at Packwood. Frequently, their owners had a powerful vision of

Three generations of the Ash family in the Hall at Packwood: from left to right, Alfred, Graham Baron and Joseph

The ivy-smothered Terrace Walk, as photographed by Country Life in 1902

the past which produced a complete work of art, extending to repairs, additions, interiors, gardens and wider setting. John Cornforth writes: 'Of course there was an element of escapism about them that some people today find hard to accept, a sense of borrowing from history, and their owners would have been aware of that.' Perfection was achieved only by using old material to fill in gaps left when such houses had fallen into decay, or been reduced to the status of farmhouses. At Stoneacre in Kent, Aymer Vallance even imported large elements of North Bore Place in Kent to form new wings and supply missing details, before he handed his idyll over to the National Trust in 1928.

The Society for the Protection of Ancient Buildings, founded by William Morris in 1877, had always taught that one old building should not be 'improved' at the expense of another. Its campaign came to a head between the wars with the architectural depredations of Randolph Hearst on a titanic scale for his Gormenghast-like castle at St Simeon in California. But preventative legislation did not come until 1947. Following the country house demolitions of the 1950s, the supply of good-quality fittings virtually dried up. Even so, the art form of the 'perfect English house' has continued to be stimulated by *Country Life*. The building of Meols Hall, Southport, as its owner felt it should have been, but never was, or the return of Stedcombe House, Axmouth, to its precise appearance of 300 years ago provide dramatic examples from recent decades of a concept that retains its appeal as strongly as ever.

TRANSFORMING PACKWOOD

At Packwood, Graham Baron Ash carried his father along with his aim to rid the house of its Georgian and Victorian work in order to re-create the sort of atmosphere which might have existed in John Fetherston's time. He followed the fashion of his day in using old material from demolished buildings to achieve this. This was the age of the re-created 'period room', when panelling and chimneypieces were treated as moveables for sale to the connoisseur. The results he achieved are typical of the most thoughtful work of the pre-war period, and the date is instantly recognisable because of the particular mixture of imported panelling continental stained glass and old textiles.

What is so remarkable about Packwood is that Baron Ash started with virtually a clean slate indoors – the main house had been so much altered that only the roof structure survived in anything like its Elizabethan or Jacobean state. The timber-framed walls had been rebuilt in brick, and the windows were mostly Georgian gothick. The interiors were not in any sense distinctive or artistic.

Without much in the way of original features as a starting point, Baron Ash needed to import historic pattern and craftsmanship:

> I do this as an antidote to the decay and demolition of so many old houses all over the country. I am rescuing whatever I can from other places and preserving it here. Of course, there are many examples of 'over' restoration and I am proceeding with the utmost caution. I hope that my efforts will not provide the antiquarian of the future with an object lesson of what *not* to do in restoring an old house!

In fact he exercised considerable connoisseurship, judging well the scale and type of early chimneypieces appropriate to each room. He would have appreciated the great rarity of the chevron-pattern floorboards reused in the entrance hall. These were from the most tragic demolition sale of the 1930s – the long semi-abandoned mansion of Lymore Park, Montgomeryshire, where the end was signalled by the indignity, for the owner Lord Powis, of the ballroom floor subsiding during a dance. So there was a romantic story to tell, too.

Connoisseurship was also demonstrated in the furnishing of the new rooms. Much research on furniture had been published in the earlier years of the century, culminating in Macquoid and Edwards's *Dictionary of English Furniture* in three magisterial volumes in 1924. Old textiles were preferred, where possible, to give colour and romance to the interior, and here the latest work was H. C. Marillier's *English Tapestries of the 18th Century* (1930). The limited supply of tapestries in presentable condition, coupled with their fragility, has since restricted their appeal for most post-war interiors. Baddesley Clinton nearby was a good local quarry for fine unaltered furniture and tapestries in the 1930s, when Cecil Ralph Ferrers was attempting to delay the inevitable day he would have to sell that estate. Had Baron Ash not bought the cream of the Baddesley collection privately, most of these treasures would probably be gone from the area.

(Left) The late 17th-century Brussels tapestry of a water garden in the Great Hall

(Right) Baron Ash transformed an old barn into a traditional Great Hall furnished with old tapestries

Queen Mary visiting Packwood in 1927

LIFE AT PACKWOOD

Though the rooms may look like museum-pieces, they were intended for everyday occupation and entertaining, and needed to be kept smart: the vogue for shabby decay had not yet arrived. As Charles Lines points out, 'No detail was overlooked – the right curtains, the correct placing of every chair, the precise and exquisite laying of a table. To stay at Packwood – housekeeper, butler, footmen in attendance – must have been rather like staying in a royal residence.' Indeed, the exquisitely remodelled house came into its own in 1927, when Queen Mary paid a visit which introduced a host of new historical associations to the house that were carefully recorded: the teacup she used is displayed in the Drawing Room. The climax of Baron Ash's life at Packwood was in 1938, when he was appointed High Sheriff of Warwickshire, fulfilling an ancient office in harmony with the antiquity of the place. Though still retaining some judicial responsibilities, it had become more of a ceremonial position than when Thomas Fetherston held it. The gardens were opened for good causes, and there were open-air Shakespeare performances.

In 1948 Baron Ash moved to Wingfield Castle in Suffolk, where he again restored an ancient house but passed the rest of his life in seclusion at that remote and beautiful place. A newspaper article of the late '50s states, 'It is never open to the public. Mr Ash told a reporter that while he was doing all he could to improve and preserve the property for posterity, he had already given one house to the nation fully furnished and endowed, and he felt that he was entitled to privacy in his present home.' Late in life, in 1967, he had a major auction of its best contents and, somewhat astonished and buoyed up by the prices realised, took pleasure in completing its furnishing all over again.

At Packwood, the ensemble survives just as Baron Ash left it over half a century ago. Not only do the rhythmic planting schemes he devised for the spectacular borders continue, but the furniture is kept where he placed it, smartly and brightly polished, supplemented as he wished with numerous cut-flower arrangements. The visual achievement is an old house looking its best in a splendid well-kept garden and wider setting. It is approachable – its small scale probably helps – stimulating and enjoyable for thousands of visitors each year. It is a celebration of all that is most beautiful about this part of Warwickshire, so richly wooded but only just sufficiently shielded from the noise, bustle and values of modern day-to-day life.

Packwood's (re)creator and his lifestyle are harder to come to grips with. The products of the industry which provided his fortune were never to be mentioned, and his social position as a gentleman, bolstered by pettinesses (anyone arriving even a second late for an appointment was sent away), was everything. It is sad that very few people could really get to know this shy and deeply knowledgeable connoisseur, who remained aloof and something of a mystery even to his own family. Of all his wide interests, the only one he would proclaim in *Who's Who* was shooting.